AF354485

To my father, you did the best you could
To my mother, you taught me the love for the written word
To all the people that have come and go into my life, and specially,
to those who inspired these lines; to all the experiences that you
brought, positive and negative, that have made me grow into the
person I am today.

A SMALL PREFACE

The world and its society have been getting more complicated over the centuries; as a species, we have achieved an enormous development of science, economy and interrelations at a worldwide level that not too long ago would have been thought as sci-fi. But as we evolve other problems appear, problems in the way we present ourselves as individuals, and as part of the group; in an age where we have (in first world societies, there's still a huge gap of inequality to solve) everything we would like in the palm of our hands the quest of the self and self-definition remains. Who are we, where are we headed, those questions bother everyone, ones more than others, in a world we have modified so much that we have become almost isolated from the natural environment and from our fellow humans.

Social interaction can have a huge impact in one being and, combining all these factors together we find that the development of conditions from the anxiety disorders and depressive disorders branches are on the rise.

Terms like *anxiety disorder* or *depression* still carry with them a not so invisible stigma of seeing the pity in other person's eyes when they look at you, or even to not be taken seriously because your perception of the real world is not *quite realistic,* so it all usually stays inside. Sadly, it's not a topic of which we can freely talk with anyone without being mocked.

Sometimes the hardest part is letting go of the grief, of all the negative things that are inside you, but as I realized that I *truly* wanted to feel good, that I *deserved,* I started to realize other subtler problems that affected (and still do) my life in a bigger way than my mood and those were my communication problems, the difficulty of translating my fast thinking onto words; and my inability to identify what I was feeling and what caused it; and so I started to sit down and write any small situation that upset my tranquillity in any way, to try and understand myself and my mental condition better.

In all the years that have passed by, and even after accepting that fact, I couldn't speak about any of this, I grew so used to wear my armour of pretending that nothing was wrong, that I was strong, capable and immovable no matter what that I could not find in me the strength of talking about it. In my eyes, it made me appear weak.

And of course, there's the situation that usually happens with mental conditions that *you think you are the one at fault,* that you are the one wrong; that you're just making a fuss over something that is totally irrelevant for other people and that your feelings and thoughts are totally *unjustified*

But here I am, doing my best at normalizing it, and I think it's up to us to open about it everyday, to show ourselves in our best and in our worst.

It's been a long journey of four years and it is one that will never conclude as long as I, or any of you, dear readers, stay alive in this confusing world and keep learning and growing, transforming ourselves as in the old art and science of alchemy; *turning lead into gold*

LEARNING TO LIVE

*Because it's difficult to be in the world when you don't
know how to be alive in the first place*

Useless

A word, a look, a stupid thought.
I try to do my best, be my best, what is expected of me.
How can I live like this? Impossible.
I must do something, I must be better, I must achieve it.

I can't.
I cannot survive in this world.

Come on, you can, this is only a momentary feeling.
It is impossible.
Calm down, be patient.
I am depending on others.
Your time will come, just don't let yourself be engulfed by this.
I cannot. I've got to be self-sufficient and I.Can't.

I am in the bed covered by my protective blanket.
Useless.
I try that no one hears me cry, I just want to submerge in here.
Useless.
My ribcage feels totally hollow, like the emptiness of the universe.
Useless.
My hands hurt, my palms sting.
Useless.
I just want to disappear.

NO!

Don't despair, come on, calm down, it's nothing, it's just one more day.
Useless.
You know it will be over, that you just feel this now, that then later you will have your strength back.
Useless.
Come on, breathe.
Useless.

Under the blanket, for a second, I disappear. I can dream that I'm not here, and turn off, for a few moments, the dialogue between two equally strong and certain parts of my brain.

Tomorrow I will be better.
Even if I remain useless, good for nothing, unable to fend for myself.

Broken branches

My heart grows like a tree, its branches intertwined, keeping
in each recess a small part of what makes
myself, of what I love or desire,
of my loved ones.

As little singing bird nests, I welcome among my branches
those persons who reach my trunk, with a "knock, knock"
they catch my attention, whatever the reason.

And so, I raise them, to my branches.

As time passes by, the greater the connection,
the desire to be with these persons, more branches I
provide for the nest,
to make their stay in this small tree-heart as comfortable as
possible.

Sometimes, however, we do not have the same concept of
sharing or affection. They're pulling at my branches. And
they hurt me.

They try to mould to their liking the nest that I provide for
them in my heart, accommodating what they want how they
want, pruning or growing to their convenience, to their need.

I don't share my nests out of necessity but because I wish so.
Why don't they realize that they are not in my tree-heart
because I need them, but because I have decided to share
myself and my branches with them?
I do not need you.

Sometimes, my branches are not very strong, and those people can fall through some gap in them.

Sometimes even if I don't need them, I still love them. And my branches are too tangled in their nests. Too much. I can't let go; I can't let them fall.
But I know I can't keep them there

So sometimes I have to severe my own branches to let those people out of my tree-heart. The nests that they thought were theirs, those that they didn't realize I provided for them, ended up on the ground, and they left

And so, my tree-heart has parts that will never grow back. Because those branches that I cut will always be with them, wherever they are.

Modern forest

There is a blue sky, full of clouds. Or it can be a night sky, full of stars.

Laying on my back, looking at the infinite; to everything at once and nothing in particular.
I observe the skies, day and night, searching for shapes on the passing clouds, joining points between the visible stars. Asking myself, from time to time, if that cloud wouldn't be in fact a mystical being, an eagle or a dragon; if that star whose light reaches us is still existing, if the other one that flickers will do so because its fuel is running out or because there is some planet orbiting around it.

I am on a rooftop, surrounded by houses, in the middle of the modern forest.
Its modern forest trees surround me everywhere: they are the antennas, those ugly things, with a metal stick like a stem, two rectangular grilles for petals and in the middle three skewer-stamens.
A real flower, if I am allowed the sarcasm.

It keeps bothering my brain, the insidious question, is it necessary? Is it really a damn antenna needed in every damn house? Is there no way to have less? Really?

The human being is harmful. And I keep remembering that quote by Rousseau "What would it be like to walk the world without industry, without speech, without a home?" What would the world be like if we humans hadn't existed? What would it be like if we had been more farsighted? Could we have developed technologically to the current level without the destruction we have generated in the process? Is there a way to fix it, now?

I'm getting tired of having to look at the sky amidst the modern forest.
I'm going to watch TV.

Hypocrite

Lies … pious lies?

I know you lied to me, there in the garden.

At that time I was so in in my own paranoia that I had
forgotten all those things you came to tell me, I was at that
point where the only way to recover sanity is breaking with
everything and leaving.
Precisely what I was doing. Because I had been so gone
before, and the symptoms can never be forgotten.

So I did the smart thing: give up; not thinking in terms of
winners or losers but in my happiness, in my mental health.
That other time I made the mistake of getting involved in a
battle of pride, but I know now where it leads, and I simply
withdrew.

And at that precise moment, when I needed it most, you came.
To have the conversation I needed; to tell me the things I had
to hear. To say what your mother had already tried, with the
difference that you knew the words you had to use with me.

Imagine my perplexity when I discovered that you lied to me;
because your words helped me, a lot. But they were a lie.

And I, who value truth above all, felt both disappointed and
confused because, how could it be, if you had lied to me, how
could those words help me so much?

And since then I reflect and think, that perhaps truth or lie are abstract concepts, that maybe at some point in the universe or in some other dimension lies are truths; or perhaps what matters is the impact that our words can make.

Maybe a lie can help people.
But yet again, the truth always prevails, just as I discovered that you had lied to me.
And it wasn't a reason strong enough to prevent your words from helping me.

Laughter

Two persons tell anecdotes,
catching up on the events of their lives.
They haven't seen each other for a long time, and there are
many things to tell; especially fun things or strange
occurrences.
There are many cackles.

A group of friends comment on what happened in the week,
student chores, quarrels with teachers, plans.
Young people without a worry about the uncertain tomorrow,
with just the thought of having fun.
There are many cackles.

The ladies who cross path every day talk about their daily
routine, they saw each other less than 24 hours ago but it
doesn't matter,
their life is bustling, always full of worries, always taking
care of their families. Surely they're talking about their
adorable grandchildren.
There are many cackles.

I go down the street, on my way to my daily tasks, I see faces
of people although I try, as always, not to focus on them; It's
the Law that we use since we were children: If we don't look
at them they won't look at us either.

I pass by two people sitting on a terrace, having a coffee,

although I try to divert my attention, I hear the laughter.

They are not laughing at me, I remind myself. *They are having their own conversation.*

With that phrase as a mantra in my mind, I meet a group of kids who are undoubtedly taking their time out of class, I see them from afar so when they reach me I do all I can to ignore them, I still hear the laughter.
Are they laughing at me? They are talking on whispers among themselves, so maybe yes, they are laughing at me.

At the exit of the supermarket there are two ladies chatting about their lives, walking next to them I try by all means not to notice, but I still hear the laughter.

And I can't stop thinking that they are laughing at my life, at any gossip they have heard and believed; of any piece of conversation about private topics that they have heard me keep with close people.
They are laughing at me.

Protective shield

There is a strong bass rhythm, very deep;
a frequency that resonates with me, or I do with it,
as if I immersed in an ocean, infinite and increasingly darker.
I focus on it to maintain sanity; it's the only thing that keeps
paranoia at bay.

Music.

I have even thought about the songs that I'm going to hear,
depending on what I'm going to do or where I'm going to go;
earphones ready before leaving home, finger on the "play"
button of my mobile player, ready to activate my protective
shield, the armour that allows me to survive in this world,
among people.

Dum Dum, Dum Dum.

Like the sound of an eternal heart, begging to be heard.
Synchronize, synchronize.
The sound is like a drop, falling over the centre of a pond,
forming waves throughout my body, from head to toe.

Focus on me

Think only on the music, don't hear anything else.
There's nothing else; only music and me.

The rest of the Universe is a deep black to float in. There are
no people, no sounds, no half-understood conversations.
Don't listen.

It's none of your business, don't listen to them, just listen to the beat, the sound.

Only the beat matters.
Only this chant.

I make them mine, until the beat is my heart, the melody my blood, the chorus my breath.

There is nothing else inside this bubble that oxygenates me in the midst of an irrespirable, hostile world,

Just me and music.

Why so serious?

In a world of duties, everyone tries to comply. Everyone strives incessantly to have a valued study, a stable job, the money to afford at least a vacation every summer, a car, home ownership.

Have children. Why? Well, because if you don't, you are not worthy of being taken seriously, it has nothing to do with wanting to be a good fatherly figure and devoting yourself to making the kids happy,
it's just what you should do.

Have friends and go out have fun with them, please. How can it occur to someone to be happy alone, or spending the night at home instead of in a nightclub?

Behave.

The ads, those stupid stereotyped recreations
designed to pour through your throat products you can't afford or actually don't need, they will tell you to be different, transgressive, to live; but the reality is very different.

If you think, even for a moment, to do what they say to take advantage of life, everyone will point at you, they will look at you over the shoulder with contempt. And that's the only control mechanism that is needed to keep you in your place, because it is so important to be an accepted member of society;
It is extremely important that you have no reason to feel ashamed of your fellow human beings.

So follow your grey routine, wondering for a moment what it would be like to act as you wish, and quickly suppressing the thought for fear that it has been minimally noticed for the other ghosts who follow their routine just like you.

You are called sane, we are the others, *the crazy ones*. We are the ones who don't care about the consequences, or at least we cope with them if what we get is to be happy in this short life, without harming anyone.

You can spend your life being afraid of what other people will think; Only oneself can live within their own body, in their own life with their unique circumstances.

Just take serious things seriously, and only oneself can decide what are the serious things.

They call us crazy because we are not afraid to do what makes us look like it. And from time to time, even for sane people, it doesn't hurt to not take life too seriously and do some craziness.

Impotence

I am on the ground, unable to move,
I try by all means to hold back tears.
It's getting more difficult by the moment.

It is stupid, it is irrational.
There will always be situations that I can't control, and yet, I
let situations control me.

Is it the rage of knowing that I can't do anything?
Or does it really affect me?
I don't understand, I don't think I'll ever come to understand
why I feel this way.

My mind doesn't work.

I would like to be a normal person, with a normal brain,
a person whose body would not collapse, would not remain
motionless,
without responding to the orders given.
I would like to be a person who was not affected by
something as absurdly ridiculous as noisy pyrotechnics.
I would like not to be pathetic.

I look like a puppy.

I close my eyes trying to pass through the cloud of panic, but
like this the noises only seem more bombs and ammunition.

And I still feel pathetic thinking that I have a crisis due to pyrotechnics when there are places in the world in which they truly are noises of bombs and rifles.

In the end, I get distracted and the attack passes, but impotence will always be my traveling companion; always very little to change the situations that make me feel this rage.

And although I think about how wonderful it would be to be a normal person, with a functioning brain, I realize that this is nothing more than an illusion; that we all probably have poor brains and we go through life trying to hide it, based on an idea that we've been told is the right thing but that doesn't really exist, except in the defective brain of the person who invented it.

Don't turn it over

I've screwed up again.
It's as simple as a gesture, a grimace or a comment, a
moment of relaxation and it happens.
I've screwed up again.

I always have to keep my guard up,
always I have to calculate the consequences by the
millimetre,
and how I make people feel with those stupid slips that
escape the filter of my brain in a moment of lack of control,
or of relaxation; of not thinking.

And I behave exactly as I don't want to.
Others might see it as a sign of strength, of how hard
I am;
but all I can see is stupid behavior,
the same that hurts me when it comes from others, and
that I apply in the moment I lower my watch.

I have screwed up again.
It begins to repeat itself in my head each and every time I
have screwed up; with an unpleasant sensation anchored to
the base of my neck, like a parasite absorbing my life.

I can't stop thinking about it, again and again.

Don't turn it over, I tell myself; It's the only way to stop the
vampire thought.
Stop spinning it, the past is indelible, you can't
change it anymore.

Why worry about something beyond your control?
Stop turning it over, you're not a failure just for having a fault,
it is a tiny percentage.

Analyze the situation, find where you were wrong,
get ready.
Improve.
Get over it.

Instead of turning around uselessly an event that has
happened and period, why don't you focus on it never
happening again?

Recognize your mistake, inspect your emotions and find out
what the trigger was, how you felt.

Identify the feeling, give it a name, grasp it, understand it,
relate it to the situation.
What caused it?
This way you can develop a better strategy.

Specially, don't turn it around anymore.
Let it be and learn what you can.

Irrational

I burn.
I am burning from the heart up,
I feel it on the shoulders and on the face, and it means it's too
late.

I usually think that I have a fire inside: It can be a warm
flame, like a home that attracts people, and it can transform
into a hell that destroys everything in its way.

I get turned on, little by little, and I do not realize, I only
know that I start to feel the heat.
When I burn, it is already late.

I have lost all logic from sight, and I hate myself for it;
in my head I will repeat the events over and over again,
thinking of all the calm approaches that I could have made, in
all the control measures that I did not activate and I should, all
the phrases that I could have said and didn't say, instead of
the ones that I did.

I don't even know what triggered this stupidity,
Why can't I control myself?
I wish I was the cold and calculated person I imagine myself
to be,
instead of an irrational bunch of nerves.

I hear myself say things just meant to hurt,
and I feel stupid. Because they are stupid things,
without foundation;

only guided by that stupid pride that tells you
that those who do not stay above others are stupid.

Well, surprise, there is no prize at the end of the day for being
on top.
 You don't get paid or receive any congratulations.

The only thing that remains after is coldness.
The only thing you feel is emptiness.

When the fire calms down; it is only then when you realize
the irreparable damage that it's caused, that you have caused.

And the only thing that's left is trying to fix what you have
broken,
regroup all the pieces and try your best to recompose it.
Use that fire in a productive way, instead of destructive.

Wrath. Irrational

Make a difference

There are times when the feeling of defeat is unstoppable,
when you want to give up, if only for a fleeting moment.
Do what everyone else, be what everyone else is, what is
expected of you.
Load on your shoulders all those ridiculous expectations
generated by ridiculous rules, invented and totally arbitrary.

There are times when everything is black, and you can't stop
thinking why they don't realize the damage they do to you,
just because you don't fit in a stereotype.
I'm human. I exist. I am a living being. I am here.
I also have the desire to be loved. Understood.
Or at least, respected in my difference.

As individual sentient beings we are all unique, and for me
that is the greatest gift of humanity: Its diversity.
The interaction between all the different options creates
culture, it's been for millennia what has generated our
societies.

Why eradicate it, why cut everything by the same pattern?
Why eliminate our intrinsic beauty?

There are days when you are one step away from the cliff;
from giving up what makes you happy just because it is not
usual.
Normal means only that which is repeated most in the
environment, it has no positive or negative connotation.
It's only the most common.

And so on the edge of the cliff many found, and will find,
themselves; and some will decide that it is better to jump, and
let themselves be dragged by the gravity that are the
expectations of others, the need to order, catalogue, label; all
in beautiful square boxes.
And if that was their choice, they should never be judged by
it.

But there will be others, like me, who can't do that.
We know we would be wretched forever.
And we turn around, back to the road that always runs along
the edge of that cliff, dodging as we can the blows, the trials,
the insults, the looks.

And maybe, even if no one says it out loud, even if they agree
with the spiral of silence of the square minds, maybe between
them there's someone who for a moment admires you,
someone for whom your act means something special.
Someone who, although has nothing to do with you, thinks
that if you have the courage to do what is out of the ordinary
they can, too.

Someone for whom you make a difference.

People

There are too many people in the world;
they occupy space in a disorderly way,
they are not pleasing.

People are a problem, because for each one of those people
they are the individual and the others "the people."

For someone, we are all people.

Like those phrases used to refer to actions that we dislike:
"People this, people that". It's an impersonal way to
complain.
It's ridiculous.

Even though we feel like the last individual standing, we're all
people.

Why don't we include ourselves,
when we criticize "the people"?
After all, if we're going to complain about what annoys us in
others,
Why not do it with what annoys us about ourselves? Or that
features of ourselves that annoy other individuals for whom
we are "the people"?

It is easy to observe through the window, it is easy to open it
and shout to the world an opinion about "the people" that
nobody asked for.
It is very easy to speak badly of "the people" when the term
excludes us.

It is easy to see the speck in another's eye.

The difficult thing is to look in the mirror,
knowing that it is only you who's looking back; the one
who makes the mistakes, the only one who is to be blamed.
The one who criticizes in others precisely the behaviours he
does.

Inherently, we all look for other's failures that we ourselves
commit, consciously or not.
Perhaps our psyche seeks them insistently because, if they are
in others, we may not feel so bad about it, because then we're
able to say "See? I am not the only one."

Finding a justification, however poor, for our behaviour,
because everyone wants their life to change, but nobody
wants to change the way they live.

Sorrow of many is consolation of fools.
You are people. Act accordingly

Suicidal

In every house there is a drawer with medicines in it, in the
bathroom, in the living room, it doesn't matter, It is the place
where medicines and various pills are stored.

Today I surprised myself looking at that drawer, thinking if it
could be something there that, taken in a high dose,
deleted myself forever.

It had been a while since this happened to me, dreaming of
having a pill to cause an overdose,
with which to die in the midst of delicious deliriums.

These feelings have always accompanied me,
since I have sense of self;
the days when you just couldn't not cut yourself, just a little
bit,
enough to feel that pain that makes you stronger.
Adrenaline, reminding the system that it is alive.

I used to think I was a coward, because I never had courage to
go until the end.
Now I know that coward is the one who gives up on life,
That the real courage is being here when you don't want to.

That doesn't stop me from having these days.
Days in which if I felt empty, if I lay hidden from the world
it would be easy. No.

The emptiness is comfortable, in it it's possible to float.

These days are full of little details, a thousand thoughts per
second,
drowning in the everything they form.
You put a façade, and you lie, and don't stop, never stop.

You have to distract, entertain yourself, because the Beast
stalks you,
waiting for the precise moment when you stop for a
moment to jump over you, to crush you with its immense
claw that doesn't allow you to breathe. Making you look at
that drawer.

I survive another day, with an eye put on ending soon;
a strange hope that breaks when a new thought appears:
What if I live up to be an old woman? What if I don't die
soon?
Would I be able to continue surviving if I knew
that many years of existence still await me?

I am still trying to reconcile with that idea.

THOUGHTS

Caged bird

I would like to sing as if I were free,
no matter what, without worrying about anything.

I want to tweet to the world,
fluttering my feathers, revelling in the air and rain,
Like a squeaky bird

Caged birds don't sing.

Maybe humans like their voices, and when they sing
they are next to them,
staring at them, delighting; But they
don't know that.
The birds can only perceive those immutable eyes on them.

But everyone knows that caged birds don't sing.

They may stop doing it for the same reason as I did, they may
feel observed, scrutinized to the smallest detail,
awaiting to be judged stupid and pathetic;
and contrite, they get engrossed in their own reality, a reality
that narrows like the bars of the cage.

I want to dance on top of a mountain,
I want to sing to the forest.

I would like to be strident, howling loudly, without
contemplations.

Dance in inexplicable and ridiculous waddles, understandable
only to me.

Raise my voice, my body and my soul in a
meaningless cacophony.
Where no one hears my voice;
where nobody can see me.

I hate you

I don't know how I can hate you so much,
just seeing you, that feeling awakens in me,
despite all the years that have passed since we met, since I
hated you for the first time.
Despite all the time we have spent interacting,
In spite of all this I am still unable to stop feeling this way.

I hate you with all my being.
I hate you

I hate you because I noticed you
because you had that something special and magical.

I hate you for all the hours we've spent talking,
of science, magic, the universe and human nature.

I hate you for your curiosity, because you don't mind asking
me about
those things you don't know, for wanting to know new
things.

I hate you for teaching me so many things that I didn't know,
real things, unlike the data that is stored in my head.

I hate you for seeing me in my lowest moments,
for being by my side while I cried rivers or exploded like a
volcano.

I hate you for hugging me and kissing me every day, for
dancing and singing with me like two crazy people.

I hate you for trying hard, for trying to make me happy.
I hate you for making me laugh even when I'm angry.

I hate you for making me emotional even when I'm writing
this,
alone, in the adjoined room, while you sleep.

I hate you because I fell in love with you.
I hate you because I love you.

I love you.
I hate you.
I love you.
I hate you.
I hate you.

I love you.

Equals (Similar)

An event has happened to me again,
of those which leave me all day rethinking what
happened.
In this case, there is a comment, and a sly smile,
half hidden, that I don't understand.

It makes me think that person has laughed at me,
has laughed at some private joke at my expense.
In this case, it is a person with whom I have always
maintained friendly, superficial interactions, yes, but non
violent in any case.

I don't get it.
I left, running, with an unusual fury that I didn't
understand
at the time.
Why am I in such a bad mood all of a sudden?
As always, I put all the blame on me and my personality.

It took me all day looking at the situation from different
angles
to realize that this person, apparently kind,
or considered not harmful on my part, he had laughed at
anything about me that seemed ridiculous to him.

With what power.
In which capacity has he considered himself worthy to judge
me

I don't get it

Why come up covertly insulting? Why come up laughing at someone?

Who, in this world of mediocre people we all are, has thought them self superior, with the power to look over the shoulder at anyone and declare that this person is worse or stupid?

Like that, out of nowhere, for no reason, simply and plainly because he had the occurrence.

Thus, he believed himself with the right and power, as if a God were, to analyse, dissect and store at his convenience.

As if all living beings on the planet didn't have the same feelings.

As if we weren't the same.

Life (shit)

Each and every day on this planet,
for each and every person on the planet, they
feel like an odyssey.

We all have a series of hopes, or ideas,
of what we should, or should have,
An expectation of reality.

And we can all mould that reality through our will, but
we all have a will, and a desire, sometimes discordant
with that of others.
The realities collide and the unexpected happens.

And so none of those wills are fulfilled, and we are left
behind,
thinking about why the Universe hates us,
why if we have worked so hard,
we don't reach those goals.

Life is bullshit, it's a truth we all know,
a certainty that makes us all sink.
Because we know we won't get it.
And it's a surge of unhappiness.

But that life is crap doesn't really mean anything. Oh
yes, we could let ourselves be dragged down, and we
will do it on black days,
but those days are as many as we can say:

I'm happy.

None will ever have any of that life planning, and
planning life is of no use.

The inexplicable, the absurd and the unexpected are there,
around the corner waiting for the right moment,
to jump in front of our faces.

In these moments more than ever is when you have to send all
your plans to trash without gloating in misery.
Work again with what you have available. Devise new plans.
And you know that those will also be rendered useless
at some point,
but hey, we already know it, don't we?
Life is bullshit, but that shouldn't stop us from being happy.

If life behaves like crap, I say: So what?

My value in the world

Once upon a time there was a bright student.
She had always had great ease, she didn't even have to
make an effort, and everyone thought she would have a
great future ahead.

When the crucial time came, to pursue the higher studies, she
decided not to take that route and everyone was very
surprised, although she was determined to pursue her other
dreams, those of a more artistic branch.

With the passing of time, the landscape was changing, the
economy sank, the university no longer guaranteed a stable
job, and all her former colleagues were having some problems
to continue with their dreams.

She herself was also having trouble making her artist dream
come true, she herself stood in her way and there isn't worse
enemy than that.

In the end, the dream was suspended for the moment, the age
had passed for that kind of thing and now it was about trying
to make a dent in the working scene, something as difficult as
the above.

And every day she thought, that maybe she should have taken
advantage of her natural talent instead of doing what she
really wanted, at least that way she wouldn't have to make any
effort, everything would have been easier, she wouldn't have

stayed in a limbo between situations, too older or too young, many studies or poorly qualified, unable to continue studying and without job opportunities.

Those days were hard, until she realized that while the others were studying she had been learning the most fundamental thing there is:
To live.
Finally, after so many years and, although it was not in a perfect way, she had learned what had always cost her the most. Now she knew how to be alive.

And so she understood that the value of a person can never be measured by the level of their studies, by the position they occupy or the money they get.

The education system does not teach you, it only makes you repeat concepts.
Jobs come and go as fast as the wheel of fortune spins.
Money's only purpose is to be exchanged for goods.

The true value of people lies in themselves, in how they always are and behave, being at the top or in the pit.

FREE STANDING

Baby steps with shaky legs will still bring you to your destination, and if you cannot even walk, just drag yourself through 'till you make it

Summer night dream

Oh, how sweet the honey of the dream!
With his golden wings of Greek God he brushes the human
soul,
plunging him into all kinds of wild adventures.

Oh, wonders of the lucid dream!
For those who are blessed with the Gift, the same they can fly
than eat the most delicious of all strawberry cakes in
existence.

But Oh, wonder, don't you turn into a nightmare!
So, just as the lucid dreamer eats the aforementioned
delicious strawberry cake, he can find that at any moment he
opens his eyes in his room.

In the dark.

Without the brain being fully awake.

And lo here, Oh Hypnos, Oh Phobos; Oh, Gods of the Dream
might you be real or emerging from the vagary of the human
mind!
That there, in the middle of the room and approaching
inexorably is a creature that should not exist in reality.

A shadow taller than the room leaning over the dreamer;
A wendigo walking on all fours towards the foot of the bed;

A portion of pillow that suddenly turns into a spider; A semi
intangible arm appearing from nowhere.

And oh, poor dreamer!

That in that moment of being the brain asleep, but not the
body, he has no other choice but to shout, until his own
screams wake him up, discovering between cold sweats that,
once again, there was nothing there.
Only the shadows of his brain.

Dream, dreamy dreamer,
Dream your reverie dreams,
full of winged pirouettes and the sweetest delicacies;

Dream without hitting yourself, without being pierced with
needles,
Dream only the scent of the unnamed fragrance that memory
brings you.

Dream without waking sleeping in the dark.

Four years

It's been four years
One doesn't notice the passing of time until it has already
gone away.
Four years.

I open the window of the car and its unique scent assaults
me,
a mix of ilex, cork oak, eucalyptus, pine trees, chestnuts,
rosemary and fruits. A common conjunction of florae easily
found anywhere but that here, somehow, produces an
irreplaceable smell.

I felt like a child again and too old at the same time

Puppeteer

Puppeteer, cut your ropes.
The doll broken, the threads loose.

So much time handling her will. My will.
So much time following your steps…

And now you go away
And you don't come back Where
are you?

Damned puppeteer, cut your ropes. You should had never get
me entangled in them if you thought about leaving me.

Broken doll, where are you going now.
The puppeteer left. She was forgotten and alone.

Puppeteer, run. As the devil's wing, fly with your winds
beyond your captivity. Beyond your curse, fly in your wind.
Honour your name.

Puppeteer, cut my ropes. Broken and threadless doll.
Puppeteer, cut my ropes, I don't need them.

Puppeteer, set me free. You don't need ropes to tie me.
Puppeteer, release me. Wherever you go I follow you, beyond
the wind, dreams, lives and times.

Because I love you, puppeteer.

And this is how dolls fall in love.

Silence, sea and sky

Walk through the trees
by a path made of wood planks

Corema album
It makes me think about *Koré* Persephone with its fresh,
round, vivid white berries that look like pearls.

Step out of the wood, into the sand.
Remove your shoes and walk
feeling it between your toes

Sinking

Stand there, in the shore
The wind is howling
The waves are slowly coming nearer
Kissing the sand, making it wet and hard
Like a lover

The sun is starting to lower in the horizon
Giving the sea a reddish tint and the sky a violet hue

So precious

Leaves you there awed, unable to move for a minute, just
looking at everything and nothing.

Start walking, along the kissing waves your feet feeling
as light as your heart feels somewhat heavy and peaceful
at the same time.

The sand is just made of decomposed corpses of clams, of
shells reduced to dust.

Sit there, listening, your brain is quiet now, no need to think
anything.

Until the light goes completely out Until
the stars start shining
So beautiful.

Just silence, sea and sky
Just me there.

I'm not there

Don't look for me in buildings
Don't look for me among constructions of concrete and metal
Don't look for me in cities
Don't look for me amidst humans
I'm not there

Only my body is walking down those corridors
I'm not there

Look for me in the forest
Between trees, with the sun filtering through their leaves

Look for me by the ocean
Emerging from the deeps by the rhythm of the waves

Look for me at night,
when everything is quiet, watching the stars

Look for me by the river
Dancing by its soft giggling

Look for me in the wild
where I belong

That's where I really am
Even if my body is in those places where you won't be able to
find me.
Then you will really see me

Summer

Soft, flowing long gowns, gauze, chiffon, delicate lace;
powder pink, lavender, ivory, teal;
tall grass blades grazing ankles while taking a stroll
through open fields;

fluffy clouds, gentle breeze, sweet tea and freshly picked
berries;
the sound of flowing water, earth colored stones rounded by
the erosion of a river;

the red sky of a sunset after a day spent in peace and solitude;

quietness

I dream of forests at night

Dreaming

I'm back in that mood when I don't want to wake up,
when I want to stay in bed all day
I'm starting to get afraid
I don't want to go back there
I can't spend my days sleeping
I must stay in the *real* world
As much real as this is

I'm starting to feel like isolating myself again and I'm
extremely afraid
I don't want to be back at square one

I don't know if I will be able to deal with people, I'm afraid
of them now too, for no reason; I know this
things are just in my mind, I know.
I know I shouldn't let this control myself and I'm afraid that
my usual mechanisms of control and self assurance are not
working.

I really don't want to get stuck in my bed again because I feel
I can't be around people.

So please, if you see me, give me a reason
This is so extremely selfish on my part, I shouldn't be asking
anyone to be my reason to get up and try to *be* But I'm so
scared and don't know what to do so, whoever see me,
please, give me a reason.
At least until this mood fades away again, until I can handle
it again.

All I can try to say myself now is that I know for sure it will get better, I will be better. I've been there and back many times. I just hope it doesn't last much

Shadow of the moon

I feel something
I don't know what it is, but it's extremely familiar. And yet I
can't quite place it. All I know is that I've felt like this before.

When?

It is almost like the feeling of autumn The
feeling of birthday coming
Of cold weather.

It is like dusk in the mountains
Or a summer night at the beach.
It's almost like the feeling of home
but it's so misplaced to have it here, now.

Even cigarettes taste different, like those I smoked there.

I feel something
I don't know what it is
But I know for sure I've felt it before
And it brings me some kind of weird peace.

Candy

Sweets make us happy
Even to those who don't like them too much

They are inherently cute, *kawaii*
Looking at them instantly can lift your mood.
It's in their shape, their gloss

We find them desirable because they are made for children,
it's their target consumers, so candy make us feel like
children, they appeal to the child in us.

A child doesn't have to take care of anything. It's not
appealing because of the memories they might bring but
because of the feeling of not having to take care of yourself,
of living without responsibilities.
Without that nagging feeling in your gut that tells you to run
away, that you have been putting too much over your
shoulders for too long.

Sweets sell us a momentary illusion of freedom

Soft

The sun makes the land soft

I've got new clothes on today, and they're so soft

I tuck a strand of hair behind my ear, so silky to touch maybe
it's not soft, maybe are my hands the ones that are soft

Maybe is our touch what makes things soften.

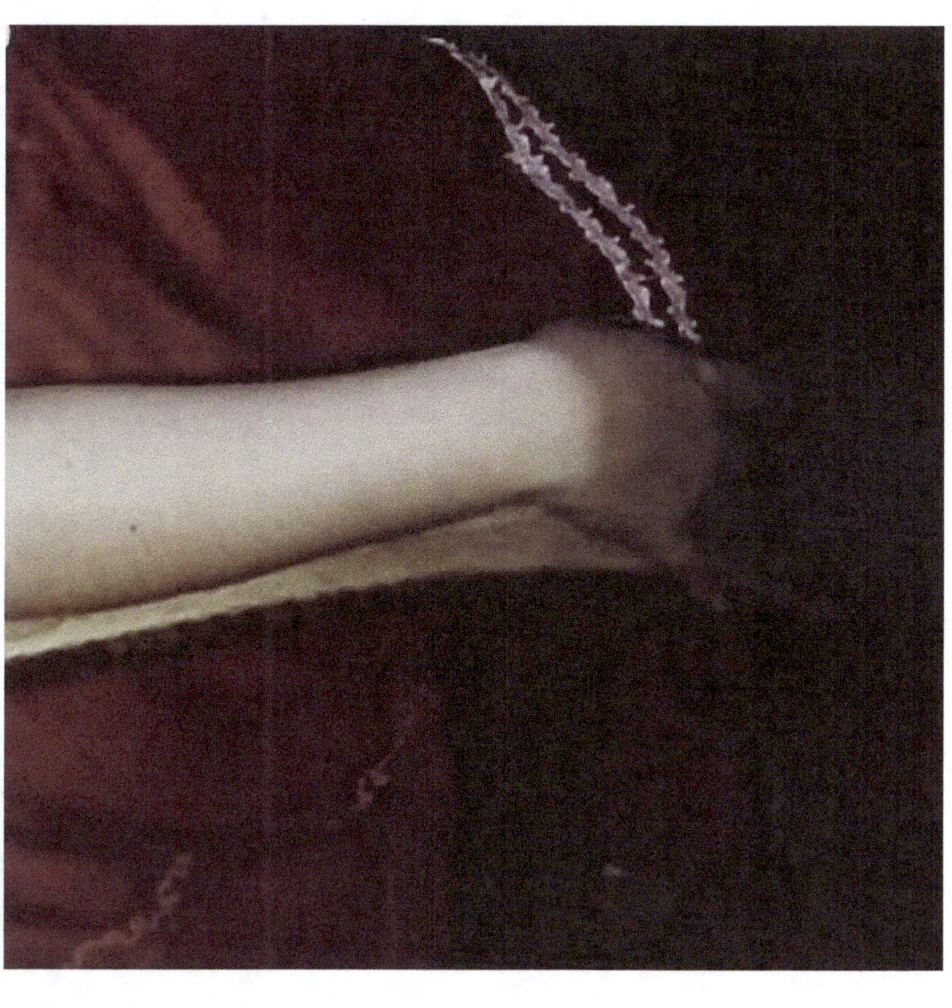

Autumn

Autumn means crisp morning drizzles,
drops carried by chilly gusts of wind;
it means cozy warm blankets, cold fingers around a cup of
hot tea.

The smell of a cake in the oven contrasting with the petrichor
scent flowing through an open window.

It means witchy hair impossible to tame, it means
Halloween,
it means shorter days that let you enjoy the darkness of the
night and in it, the brightness of stars.

It means falling asleep comfortably to the sound of rain.

RAMBLINGS OF A YEAR

Who might have thought that life would get so crazy?
Remember not to take anything as a fact, you never know where
you might end up, you just can't imagine.

Le Roman

Wouldn't it be nice, if we still lived like those first years of
the 20th century?
When people could speak many languages, and they hung out
at the homes of their equally cultivated friends chatting about
literature, philosophy, and many other things?

And I know, I probably am '*romanticizing*' things, that not
everybody could carry on that lives, only those who could
afford an education could live like that, but still, wouldn't it
be nice?

There is always someone charismatic enough to bring
together that group of people with awesome ideas,
exceptional and out of the ordinary,
and I have experienced that, meeting someone that makes you
feel attracted like a moth to a flame, more than once actually;
But you know what, that kind of people in fact end up burning
you.

And living through this adventure, traveling and working
away from home, family and loved ones makes myself
wonder if it were like this back then, meeting people that in
only two months become your friends in a way that, when
they go you know you will miss them forever, most of all
when they go and you can't even say goodbye…

But even then I still think that it would be nice to live like that
a little. Go to the theatre, opera or cinema, go once a week to
speak about everything and nothing, and write, sing, play

music, that certain way of enjoying life because it went away
far too quick.
And I think, maybe, it's not too late yet, that we could still
live like that, in our own way.

Too much

How is it possible that something so small holds so much power?

Over my thoughts
Over my acts and decisions
Small things, everyday, and then.... nothing

Nothing for a long time
It kills me
It makes me recall every moment

And think
All over again
Overthinking
Overanalysing

Trying to get a hang on what the fuck is going on Why the heck "*that*" has that power over me?
Why do I let *it* have it?
Why I don't want to say no more?

I can't stop
I must stop
I will stop

Moments

Life is made up of little moments,
of feelings that sparkle like shining, beautiful crystals, gems.
It's quartz, moonstone, amethyst.

There are exact, precise moments that get recorded in our
heart forever,
Not in our mind, never in our minds, always in our hearts, we
can remember them in a way, when you get a feeling, and you
know you've felt like that before and say "oh my gods, this is
like that time";
that's how we remember;
By scents, by sounds.

Tonight, listening again to the podcast of my favourite radio
program
Hearing again this concert live recorded, or that session by the
end of it.

I lay down, outside, and clearly remember the first night I
listened to it;
laying on a rooftop, on the floor, looking up at the night sky,
at the incommensurable, at the shining stars that may or may
not be dead already.

The coldness, the dampness in the air;
my beloved bunny, little ball of fur cleaning himself in the
dark, almost giving me a heart attack because I couldn't see
clearly what was there, and how his movements fitted so

well with that song.
Hearing for the first time that other song, so mystic and
ethereal
The feeling of peace this sounds bring to me back again.

Remembering through senses, and not through any logical
part of my brain.

Focusing in myself, coming back to my centre, as the very
small creature I am in the vastfullness of the Universe.

Life is made of moments like this,
even if we sometimes forget it.

So nice

Everybody is nice
I truly believe so, I think that they are genuine
That they really care

But anyway even if they care, at the end of the day I'm only a
number doing numbers.
And the only thing that really matters at the end of the day is
how many numbers this little number made.

I could break with it. Maybe I should.

I could get out of the game and live like a hermit forever, it
was one of my dreams after all.

Any way it doesn't matter now because the palms of my hands
are hurting, like I had a nail through them.
And I know what it means.

It's the same feeling that I always had whenever I decided to
sacrifice a part of me for the wellbeing/comfort of the people
that I care about.
It's the feeling of putting others before me.

What can I do?
I'm a desperate romantic; and the problem with us desperate
romantics is that we always do that.

No matter what

A burning heart

I thought you were like the Sun,
warming everything its rays touch, warming
everything that is around you,
ever so softly as the gentlest spark of a summer
dawn

We view the Sun through the eyes of life on the Earth, we
only see it as the thing that nurture us and
makes us grow;
But we don't fully realize its true nature.

Because you, like the Sun, are a Cosmic Fire; fiery, burning
with an unknown intensity, with a core so pure that is out of
our comprehension.

It is the fire that burns in the depths of the Hades, the fires of
the ancient temple of Heliopolis, the blue flame that test and
purify the souls.

It is Phoenix

And so are you

Unbelievable stupidity

It would be so simple
just to type a few words,
to say *hi* without any purpose,
to ask how are you,
because I'm really interested, mind you.

It should be so easy to say what I really want to say:
I miss you

I am both curious and scared as hell
What would you do?
If I told you everything,
everything that have crossed my mind and heart .
I feel so stupid.

Why didn't I spoke to you before?
Why didn't I told you all this?
Why did I have to meet you?

Why do I keep writing about this, about *you*, always, *always
about you?*
My heart is killing me,
and I know, *I know,* I can't have it both ways,
I can't be with you the way I'd *love* to.

Why did I have to meet you?

Split

I told myself so many times
That I should let you go
That you were not for me

I told myself so many times
That all I wanted was to see you happy
But the problem is, I told myself those things just to try and
convince myself of it.

I had been telling myself those things for months when I
realized it

Now. My heart is split.
Divided in two parts that pull me to opposite directions.
And I know that I can't chose both

I've tried so many times before, but maybe, maybe this is the
one time I succeed and I can take you away
from my thoughts

Maybe I can see you finally getting the happiness you deserve
From the distance

Red moon

The moon is red
She's puffy, her cheeks swollen
She lost her Sun.

She tells herself *We're still at the same place, the same
distance between us; nothing have changed, nothing....*
But still it feels like the whole Earth is between them.

The moon is red,
crying tears of Blood Because she
misses her Sun

Impossible dreams

Last night I dreamt of you again,
of you waking me up in the middle of my nightly
delirium, by kissing me.

It's always the same, blissfully unconscious and suddenly
waking up in a dream by your warm, feverish lips;
pushing your tongue in my mouth, making me softly bite
your lower lip as I regain control of the kiss.

Making the things that I would have liked to do in reality.
Being together.
Holding your hand, smile at you.

Crying when you told me not to get close to you because
you're a monster.
Crying for you, for how much I miss you.

All of my memories of you, of the moments we spent
together; it feels like they are a whole life apart, as if it all
happened ages ago, or just in a dream.

All I have of you now are no more than what this all was from
the beginning, impossible dreams that will never come true.

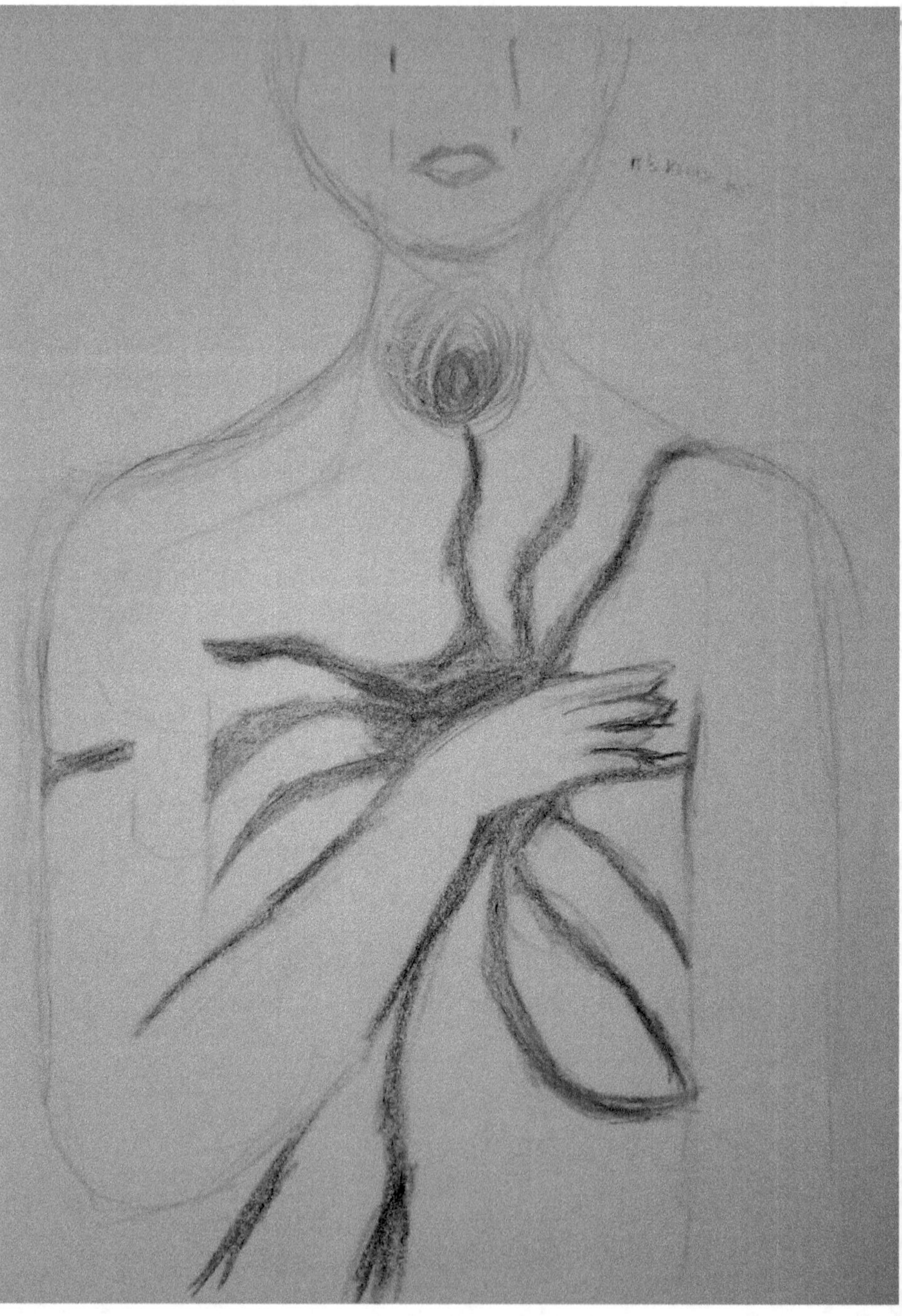

The Dam

Brick over brick
Putting more stones on this wall
to retain everything inside.

I will put up the barricades and silence my heart,
I'll listen only to my head for a long time.

My brain is crazy, but it seems it is the saner of the both.
I think if I feel anything more, only a little, a small drop, I'd
collapse

I did this to myself
It's not anyone's fault, only I'm to blame
I hurt myself

I destroyed myself, and everything around me, again.

But still there is this voice that tells me that I have done
the best,
that I'm on the right path.

I suppose that for something new to be created, for a new
period and a new cycle, the old one must be erased, crumbled
to dust.

Seeds of love

If I open up myself again
If I lay in this bed with you
How can I cope afterwards?

The water lowered, the waves recessed,
I thought it was safe enough to take a look.
I can't deny I still feel something in my chest when I look at
you but,
after I kissed you,
after I lay there with you,
the other feelings came back again;
and I realized,
that these both feelings share the same root.
If I water this plant of my love for you, I will be
reliving again the other one.

ANEW

Start all over again and again, but remember that even if it hurts, if it bleeds and burns, it means you're not dead yet.

June

It was June and I was married
It was June and I felt something strong for you
It was June and I was so confused

It was June.

With stones, with carved candles engraved with symbols, with
your name on it; with fire and paper I burnt my spell, and
wind and rain carried it away.

It was June and with stones, candles, symbols, paper, fire,
wind and rain I wished to put you on the path to achieve what
you desire.

It was June and I casted a spell to put you on the way of love
It was June and I was thinking about divorce

It was June and, for my spell I sacrificed my marriage.
It was June and I gave up my love so you could find yours.

Keep it inside

I've shed so many tears

First hopeless tears, hurtful and blaming to myself for what
I've done.
Then they became denial tears, too much to handle and too
much to block.
Finally, they've turned into bitter tears, of resentment.

I tried to be angry at you but I'm only furious with myself.

The dam I built can resist, most of the time.

Keep everything in quarantine

It was over long ago

I was dragging a corpse
for months I was pulling it, carrying its dead weight over my
back

I had tried many times to delude myself that it wasn't dead,
but I was just carrying a corpse that I didn't let go of because I
didn't want to hurt you

But it was dead, and there was no turning back

And when I finally mustered the courage to tell you I felt
miserable for hurting you
but it was the truth, it was dead.

And as much as I tried to revive it, it was not coming back to
life.

I felt miserable, yes, but at the same time I felt so light, letting
go of the dead body of that which I had proudly carried while
it was alive for so many years.

But oh, the beauty of dead things can be so charming

Don't come any closer

Don't stop
Please, *please*, don't stop
Keep your way, go on

Don't you realize that every time I'm near you you turn my
world upside down?
You didn't want me near anyway so, why would you stop
now?
Don't do it

I'm trying so hard to avoid you at all costs.
We weren't even friends to begin with.

If you stop, if you approach me *now*, everything I have
achieved will turn to dust and this nonsense would start all
over again.

Don't stop. I'm not looking at you so we can pretend we didn't
see each other.

Please, don't get close to me.

I can see you now

I saw you on the supermarket the other day.
I saw you with your girl, holding hands.

You had your eyes shining with emotion, a smile tugging on
your lips all the while you spoke to her.
I saw you like I'd never seen you before
I saw you genuinely happy, I saw you bright, not as a burning
flame as you used to, but as the fire of a home that calmly
crackles the wood and send sparkles in all directions.

And you know what? I thought I would die because of these
feelings but, since that day, my hurricane stopped, it also
stopped raining and the waves calmed back down and it
seems that now there is no risk of it flooding me again.

I think all I needed was to see you happy, so focused in her
that you didn't even notice me.

And I hope so much
I hope that you have patience with each other when trying
times come.
I hope whenever you get angry you always remember why
you fell in love with each other in the first place. I hope that
you don't try to change each other to fit in your views of how
a partner should be, but that you support each other and push
forward if that change means improving and growing as a
person.
I hope, I hope with all my heart and soul that she'd be your
forever

I'm singing your name

There it is, coming again with a mere thought, the sound of
his name.

Don't dwell on it, let it pass through you.
You know it could destroy you again.

You're now the one in control, let it flow, let him go, distance
yourself from it.

No

I am nothing
I am no one

I don't fit anywhere
I don't belong to nowhere

I don't belong
I have no place

Nowhere
No one
Nothing

Thanatos

And suddenly I realized why

I would never be happy, I can't For I am
in love with Thanatos
I always were.

But I swore to myself many years ago to leave him alone, to
not bother him anymore, to stop thinking of him and calling
his name upon my mind. To stop invoking him.

This world will never work for me, my heart will always be
restless and broken.

Such is the Fate of one in love with Death

Knowing it makes my heart flutter, light again.

Reality dawning

What am I doing with my life?

Is there even something to do with it?

Or are all those things just stupid ridiculous reasons to live
that are only valid in movies?

What if there's not really anything, what if none of us is going
to do something important, relevant?

What if…. this is really it, what if this is all that there is to
life, to be alive?

Then, why am I so unsatisfied?

I don't want to get comfortable

I *am* enough

Sometimes even the best that you have to give is not enough.

Sometimes even when you have proved yourself over and over again, you're not enough.

But now, even if they could just go along with the situation and decided not to, even if they gave me the ultimate rejection; even if I know, for sure this time, that doesn't matter what I do or what I can offer it will never be enough I *don't,* I *won't* feel less.

I *am* enough, I *do* my best. Even if it hurts, even if I feel like they stabbed me and twisted the knife even deeper, I'm not going to let this get to me.

I'll keep just....going. Wherever this crazy life decides to bring me

Coincidences

Yesterday I drew a crow
I wanted to do a watercolour style,
evoking the impression that the wet colour creates, the stain.

The crow, who was flying over us all,
and who pretended to embody the internal turmoil; in the
end it became a bird that brings the night,
and with it the brightness of the stars.

Under the drawing, I wanted to sign with a brief description,
as if giving a name to a painting, and I called my crow of
dreams
"The Bird of the Tempest"

In the end I left it unfinished, like everything I start, because I
did not get the effect I was looking for, but now, lying on the
sofa a day later my Bird of Tempest comes to mind.

Now, after a summer storm night, charged with his electricity,
his rage unleashed.

Those whom our head is constantly screaming find peace
when it is nature that is agitated in total meaningless
cacophony.

Now, after a raven has let me grab him to get him off a road
and still I feel like I did not do enough for him.

I do not think there is a reason for everything that happens in
life,
nor do I see signs in every irrelevant little detail,
but I do understand that chance creates random events that are
what promote life,

growth
change

Dead skin

I had grown and you didn't

It is so beautiful, those love stories, you and me against the
world; but it's not healthy.

We only had each other and, in our misery, we held onto it
for dear life.
But that's not healthy.

And I grew up, but you didn't
I had to shake you out, like the snake scratches free of its dead
skin.
It sounds horrible but it's the truth.

You helped me in those years, we shaped each other, but I had
outgrown you, like a snake.

And I had to get free of that skin that didn't allow me to
breath; too tight and strangling.

To pagan gods

I prayed to pagan gods
for a light to my path

I prayed to pagan gods,
to lead me in my way.

I prayed to pagan gods,
to let everything fall in place.

I prayed to pagan gods,
and you appeared.

The most curious thing of it all is that you were already there
for months, and I never noticed you until that day.

The strangest of it all is that you came when I wasn't
expecting, and when I couldn't care less about love.

The best of it all is that you are here in a time of my life when
I feel really comfortable to be in my own skin.

And you know, I prayed to pagan gods and they said "this was
predetermined".

So natural

You asked me if I was shy
no, I'm not.

But everything happened so fast that I couldn't believe it.
That I had this kind of luck, it was never part of even my
wildest dreams.

That feeling, when things fall in place so easily, so naturally,
so comfortably that it scares you

A little bit.

With intensity

Why do I have to love like this?
It's coming back again, and it hurts
the sting of love

It hurts

And I tell myself, why am I doing this again?
Why am I letting myself fall like this again?
Fall for you

Why am I allowing to let go of my control like this again?
Why am I allowing someone to have any power over
me
again?

And it hurts so much
like a thousand needles pinched around my heart
and with every move they get more stuck

Why do I have to love like this?

Red flags

I gave you the power to destroy me and you showed me
your flags,
flags that you see a carnation red
but that I can't see in such a shade.

You think your flags are so deep,
so inconveniencing and crimson, but I
cannot see them that way since they're the
same that I bear.

Maybe I'm just stupid,
maybe I'm making the same mistake again, but this
time, with you, I'm sure you deserve that I make this
mistake

That I don't see your flags so red,
since they're the same that I wear.

Don't give up

I doubt myself so hard many times
I doubt this we have.

But somehow in the midst of my worst,
lowest moments, I can't shake
the feeling that my heart is in the right place.

I've said this with others
only to be completely wrong in the end.
But somehow I keep hearing
that small voice saying
"Don't give up, don't give up on him"

Maybe I just don't want to accept the truth,
maybe I can't move on, but this feeling
tells me that my heart is in the right place.

"We create what we believe in" you said to me once
and I do believe in you
so so much.

I still love you
(even though I know it's not reasonable)

*I was so caught up in
my own warm emotions
when he put his arms around me
that I couldn't read his.*

*I should've been paying attention
maybe I wouldn't be so lost now.*

I support, no, *I back you up;*
I'll stand by your side and help you fight,
the same that you still do for me.

I'll keep putting up my smile for you,
I'll keep cracking jokes and playing fool
if that way I can bring a smile to your face.

Even if I'm unsure and broken after all this,
you haven't stopped being my friend;

You've shown me respect, pride, and instilled an unusual
inspiration and illusion in me.
You're brilliant, so much light in you even in this times
when your shadows are equally strong.

You're fascinating to me, in your lonely ways,
and I can see now that you love in other shapes,
unbeknown to me,
but that could teach me a valuable lesson,

a lesson of patience and calmness.

Even if inside I'm still craving your arms
and your warmth; this will suffice.

This will be enough.
And I will be happy to spend the time I can as a friend to you.

I'm not renouncing to who I am,
I'm not renouncing to my intensity
I'm just learning to relax a little bit.

This is new, and exciting to me.

I'm ready

www.mercureaart.com